The Morning After

While every precaution has been taken in the preparation of this book, the publisher assumes no responsibility for errors or omissions, or for damages resulting from the use of the information contained herein.

THE MORNING AFTER

First edition. November 4, 2023.

Copyright © 2023 Jeremy B. Sims.

ISBN: 979-8223115410

Written by Jeremy B. Sims.

Table of Contents

"To my mother, the beacon of strength and wisdom in my life. Your unwavering faith, resilience, and love have been the guiding stars on this transformative journey. Thank you for being my anchor and for teaching me the value of growth, even in adversity. This is for you." Happy BIrthday 70

Understanding, Addressing, and Transforming the Consequences of Our Choices

Chapter 1: Introduction

The Dawn of Reflection

In the soft, tender light of dawn, as the world begins to stir and life reawakens, many of us have found ourselves grappling with the residue of the night before. This moment – heavy with emotion, contemplation, and sometimes regret – is universally known as "The Morning After."

A Universal Phenomenon: The Concept of "The Morning After."

Every culture, every age group, every gender - no demographic - is immune to the weight of this phenomenon. From the soldier reflecting on the battle of the previous day to the teenager pondering over an impulsive decision; from the executive regretting a hasty deal to the lover reminiscing about a passionate night, everyone has had their own "morning after."

It's a shared experience that binds us as humans, making us reflect upon our actions, intentions, and consequences. This moment can be filled with a range of emotions: elation, sorrow, regret, relief, or even confusion. It's a time when the world seems clearer yet more complicated, a juxtaposition that only the human psyche can truly comprehend.

The Impact of Choices: A Brief Overview.

Life, in its essence, is a series of choices. Some are trivial, while others can alter the trajectory of our lives. But each decision, regardless of its magnitude, brings with it consequences. And often, it's in the quiet solitude of the morning after that we truly come face to face with these outcomes.

While some mornings bring with them the sweet satisfaction of choices well made, others are laden with the heavy burden of regret. It's in these moments that we question our motives, our instincts, and the very fabric of our decision-making. Why did we choose a certain path? Were we driven by impulse, desire, fear, or logic? How do these choices define who we are and who we will become?

This introduction seeks to dive deep into the heart of human behavior, emotions, and decisions. As we navigate through the subsequent chapters, readers will be invited to introspect, empathize, and, most importantly, understand the complex tapestry of choices and consequences. This is not just a book; it's a journey - a journey of understanding, reflection, and ultimately, growth.

Together, we will traverse the landscape of "The Morning After," unearthing stories, experiences, and insights that resonate with the soul, reminding us that in our moments of introspection, we are never truly alone.

Chapter 2: The Psychology Behind 'The Morning After'

Regret, Guilt, and Remorse

At the heart of many a 'morning after' is a complex blend of regret, guilt, and remorse. These emotions, though distinct in their nuances, often converge to create a cocktail of self-reflection and introspection.

- **Regret** is the recognition that one's actions led to undesirable outcomes. It's the "what if" that gnaws at our consciousness, making us wonder about alternate realities had we chosen differently.
- **Guilt** is deeper; it stems from the belief that one has violated personal or societal codes of conduct. Guilt makes us question our moral compass, pushing us to seek penance or redemption.
- **Remorse**, the most profound of the three, is a combination of regret and guilt, intensified by the empathy for those affected by our actions. It involves a deep desire to make amends.

Why do I feel this way?

The complexity of human emotions can be attributed to our evolutionary need for social cohesion and survival. When we experience regret, guilt, or remorse, it's our psyche's way of signaling that our actions might have jeopardized our standing in our social circle, which historically could mean the difference between life and death.

Immediate Gratification vs. Long-Term Consequences

The battle between the allure of immediate pleasures and the looming specter of long-term repercussions is age-old. Often, in the heat of the moment, the former wins, leading to the classic 'morning after' reflection.

- **Immediate Gratification**: Our brains are wired to seek pleasure. When faced with a tantalizing prospect, the promise of instant reward can cloud our better judgment. It's the "just this once" rationale that often leads to impulsive decisions.
- **Long-term Consequences**: As the dust settles and the high from the immediate pleasure wanes, we are left to contend with the aftermath. It's a stark reminder that every choice, however fleeting, casts a long shadow.

What was going through my mind?

The contrast of choice, often in these situations, boils down to the brain's original desire for pleasure, clashing with the more rational, forward-thinking part of our consciousness. The limbic system, responsible for pleasure and rewards, can sometimes overpower the more logical frontal cortex, especially in emotionally charged situations.

The Human Brain: Pleasure Centers and Decision-making
Understanding our actions requires a delve into the intricate workings of the human brain, especially the regions involved in pleasure and decision-making.

- **Pleasure Centers**: The nucleus accumbens, part of the brain's reward circuit, plays a pivotal role. It releases dopamine, a neurotransmitter linked to pleasure, reward, and motivation. This "feel good" chemical can sometimes lead us astray, making us prioritize short-term pleasure over long-term well-being.
- **Decision-making**: The prefrontal cortex, responsible for rational thinking and decision-making, constantly evaluates choices based on potential outcomes. When it's overruled by the pleasure centers, the result is often impulsive decisions that lead to 'morning after' reflections.

What would I have done differently?
With a clearer understanding of the brain's workings, one can develop strategies to balance immediate desires with long-term outcomes. Mindfulness, meditation, and cognitive training can enhance the brain's decision-making capabilities, making us more equipped to handle tempting situations.

As we navigate the jumble of our emotions and the workings of our brain, it's crucial to remember that every 'morning after' is an **opportunity**. An opportunity to **learn**, **grow**, and, most importantly, **understand us a little better.** Every reflection, every moment of introspection, is a step towards a more **mindful** and **conscious existence.**

Chapter 3: Exploring Addictions & Bad Behaviors

The Neuroscience of Addiction

At the core of many 'morning after' reflections is the throbbing pain of addictive behaviors. Addiction, contrary to popular belief, is not just a lack of willpower; it's deeply rooted in the intricacies of our brain's wiring.

- **Brain Chemistry**: Dopamine, the "pleasure" neurotransmitter, plays a central role in addiction. When addictive substances or behaviors are indulged in, they cause a surge of dopamine, creating a rewarding sensation. Over time, regular surges can lead to the brain becoming dependent on the substance or behavior to feel pleasure.

- **Brain Structure**: The amygdala, associated with emotions and memory, can create a conditioned response to certain stimuli leading to addictive behaviors. Moreover, the prefrontal cortex, which should regulate such behaviors, may become impaired with prolonged addictive behaviors.

- **Neural Pathways**: Repeated indulgence in addictive behaviors can carve neural pathways, making it easier for the brain to travel down these paths in the future. This means that over time, addictive behavior becomes a **default response**.

Social and Environmental Triggers
While the brain's mechanisms form the foundation of addictive behaviors, social and environmental factors often act as the catalyst.

- **Peer Pressure**: Being in a group where addictive behaviors are normalized can make individuals more susceptible. The desire to fit in or be accepted can override one's internal warnings.
- **Emotional States**: People often turn to addictive substances or behaviors as a coping mechanism for stress, trauma, or emotional pain. The temporary relief they provide can quickly spiral into dependency.
- **Environmental Cues**: Being in a setting reminiscent of past indulgences can act as a potent trigger. For example, visiting a bar where one used to drink can create a powerful urge to do so again.

Why Can't I Identify These Social and Environmental Triggers?

Recognizing social and environmental triggers is crucial in understanding and potentially altering addictive behaviors. However, several reasons might make it challenging for an individual to discern these triggers:

1. Habituation and Normalization

Over time, repeated exposure to certain behaviors or environments can make them seem "normal" or routine, even if they act as triggers. For instance, if someone is constantly around peers who indulge in addictive behaviors, they might not view it as a "trigger" but rather as a standard way of life.

2. Lack of Self-awareness

Many people go through life on autopilot, not pausing to reflect on their behaviors and their reasons. Without active introspection, it's easy to miss the underlying triggers that lead to certain actions or choices.

3. Cognitive Dissonance

Humans naturally desire consistency in their beliefs and actions. When there's a discrepancy (like knowing a behavior is harmful but still engaging in it), the brain might downplay or ignore external triggers to reduce mental discomfort.

4. Emotional Overwhelm

For someone dealing with trauma or intense emotional pain, the immediate need might be to find relief, however temporary. This urgency can overshadow the ability to recognize and analyze the triggers leading to the addictive behavior.

5. Fear of Change

Recognizing and admitting to triggers might mean that one must make significant life changes, like distancing oneself from certain friends or avoiding favorite places. This potential upheaval can be daunting, causing some to subconsciously avoid identifying triggers.

6. Minimization and Denial

It's common for individuals, especially in the early stages of addiction, to minimize the severity of their situation or deny that there's a problem at all. This defense mechanism can blind them to obvious triggers.

How to Improve Trigger Recognition

1. **Journaling**: Keeping a daily log of activities, emotions, and behaviors can help in pinpointing patterns and potential triggers.
2. **Therapy**: A trained therapist can provide an outside perspective and guide individuals in recognizing and addressing triggers.
3. **Mindfulness and Meditation**: These practices can enhance self-awareness and make it easier to identify external influences on behavior.
4. **Educate Yourself**: Understanding the science and psychology behind addiction can provide insights into personal triggers.
5. **Seek Feedback**: Trusted friends and family might see patterns and triggers that an individual doesn't recognize.

Remember, recognizing triggers isn't about assigning blame or feeling guilty; it's about **understanding oneself better and creating a path to healthier choices and behaviors.**

Case Studies: From Drugs to Gambling

To truly understand the nature and impact of addiction, it's essential to delve into real-life instances.

1. **The High Roller**: A detailed look into the life of a once-successful businessman whose casual trips to the casino turned into a compulsive gambling disorder. This case will shed light on how the thrill of the game, the environment, and personal stressors intertwined to create a destructive pattern.

2. **The Escape Artist**: The story of a young woman turning to narcotics as an escape from a traumatic past. This case will highlight the intricate interplay between emotional pain, brain chemistry alterations due to drug use, and societal pressures.

3. **The Social Drinker**: A journey into the life of an individual whose occasional drinks with friends turned into alcohol dependency. This story will underscore the role of social settings, peer behaviors, and the brain's reward system in the transition from casual drinking to alcoholism.

Case Studies: Exploring the Depths of Addiction

1. The High Roller: A Descent into Gambling Addiction

Background:

Jason was a 40-year-old businessman who once commanded boardrooms, sealing six-figure deals with confidence. Married with two children, he had a sprawling home in the city's upscale neighborhood.

The Catalyst:

A casual trip to a casino during a business convention introduced Jason to the euphoria of gambling. Winning a considerable sum on his first night, the casino environment – the flashing lights, the exhilarating sounds of slot machines, and the admiration from onlookers – was intoxicating.

The Downward Spiral:

What started as occasional visits to local casinos soon became weekly affairs. Jason began chasing losses, borrowing money to fuel his addiction, and lying to his family about his whereabouts. As the stakes grew, so did his debts.

Underlying Triggers:

Jason's business faced multiple setbacks, and he felt the mounting pressure to maintain his family's luxurious lifestyle. Gambling became an escape – a realm where he felt in control, even when he was losing. The casino's environment only amplified his desires, providing a space where he felt valued and successful.

2. The Escape Artist: From Pain to Pills

Background:

Lila, a 23-year-old college graduate, had her life upended by a traumatic incident in her late teens. Trying to piece her life back together, she moved to a new city for a fresh start.

The Catalyst:

To cope with the relentless flashbacks and nightmares, Lila was prescribed pain medication after a minor car accident. The pills didn't just numb her physical pain – they dulled her traumatic memories too.

The Downward Spiral:
Lila started increasing her dosage, using the drugs as a crutch to escape her traumatic past. She isolated herself from friends and family and began purchasing narcotics off the street when her prescriptions ran out.

Underlying Triggers:
The trauma from her past remained unaddressed, making narcotics an appealing escape route. The initial legal prescription gave her a false sense of the drugs' safety, and societal pressures to appear "okay" made her hide her growing dependency.

3. The Social Drinker: From Toasts to Trouble
Background:

Mike, a 29-year-old marketing executive, was known for his charisma. Active in his city's social scene, he was often the life of the party.

The Catalyst:

Mike's social circle often met at bars and pubs, where rounds of drinks were customary. Over time, these rounds became more frequent, and the quantities larger.

The Downward Spiral:

Mike began drinking outside of social settings, using alcohol to unwind after work. Slowly, he needed alcohol to start his day, and then to keep it going. He would brush off friends' concerns, labeling himself just a "social drinker."

Underlying Triggers:

The societal norm of drinking in his social circle blurred the lines between casual consumption and dependency. Professional pressures and a desire to always be the jovial, carefree center of attention made him turn to alcohol as a consistent companion.

These cases highlight the complex interplay of personal, societal, and environmental factors that can drive individuals into the clutches of addiction. Recognizing these stories in ourselves or those around us is the first step towards understanding and healing.

As we traverse the complexities of addiction and bad behaviors, it becomes clear that these issues aren't black and white. There's a vast gray area influenced by biology, society, and personal experiences. Recognizing and understanding these nuances is the first step towards compassion, both for ourselves and for others. Every 'morning after' reflection stemming from addiction is a plea, a call for help, understanding, and a desire to break free.

Chapter 4: Sex, Relationships & 'The Morning After'

Casual Encounters and Their Impact

The evolution of modern dating, fueled in part by technology and shifting societal norms, has led to an increase in casual encounters. While some find empowerment and freedom in such experiences, others face emotional turbulence, confusion, or regret.

Why Do Casual Encounters Happen?

1. The Quest for Freedom and Exploration

In an era where individualism and autonomy are highly valued, many people see casual encounters as a form of personal freedom. They provide an opportunity to explore one's own desires, preferences, and curiosities without the constraints of a committed relationship. These encounters can serve as a playground for discovering what one likes, wants, or needs from intimate relationships, free from long-term expectations or responsibilities.

2. Modern Societal Dynamics and Technology

The proliferation of technology, especially dating apps, has revolutionized how people meet and interact. These platforms offer convenience and a vast pool of potential matches, allowing for swift and frequent connections. Coupled with a fast-paced society where many prioritize career or personal growth over settled relationships, the stage is set for more casual liaisons. These encounters can fit more seamlessly into lives that are in constant flux or transition.

3. Emotional Coping and Validation

Casual encounters can also stem from deeper, often unacknowledged emotional needs. For some, the fleeting intimacy provides a temporary salve for wounds like low self-esteem, loneliness, or past traumas. The affirmation gained from being desired, even for a night, can offer a potent boost to one's self-worth. However, this can be a double-edged sword; while some find genuine comfort and pleasure, others might later grapple with feelings of emptiness or regret.

4. The Biological Imperative and Thrill of Novelty

From a biological standpoint, humans are hardwired to seek out novel experiences. Novelty triggers the release of dopamine, a neurotransmitter associated with pleasure and reward. New intimate partners can activate these dopamine pathways, making casual encounters exhilarating. Moreover, evolutionary theories suggest that diversifying potential mates could have reproductive advantages, a primal drive that might still subtly influence modern behaviors.

5. Societal Norms and Peer Influences

Society and peer groups play undeniable roles in shaping behaviors. As societal norms shift, behaviors that were once taboo become more accepted, and vice versa. For some, casual encounters are normalized by their social circles or the media they consume. Being in environments where casual relationships are frequent and normalized can make them seem like an attractive or even expected option.

In understanding why casual encounters happen, it's crucial to recognize the blend of personal motivations, biological drives, and external influences. Every individual's reasons are unique, shaped by a mosaic of internal feelings and external pressures.

Physical and Emotional Consequences: Not all casual encounters are emotionally neutral. They can range from being exhilarating and confidence-boosting to causing feelings of emptiness, sadness, or regret. Physically, apart from the risk of STDs, there's the added dimension of potential unwanted pregnancies.

Attachment and Detachment: The body releases oxytocin, often dubbed the "love hormone", during intimate encounters. This can lead to feelings of attachment, even in casual settings, potentially complicating emotions post-encounter.

The Psychological Reasons Behind Risky Sexual Behaviors

Venturing into the realm of intimate relationships, many factors influence decisions, sometimes pushing individuals towards risky behaviors.

- **Seeking Validation**: For some, engaging in intimate acts becomes a way to seek validation and affirmation of their desirability or worth.

- **Impulse and Instant Gratification**: The rush of the moment, fueled by alcohol, drugs, or sheer adrenaline, can overshadow judgment, leading to impulsive decisions.

- **Traumatic Responses**: Past traumas, including previous abusive relationships or experiences, might lead some to dissociate from their actions, resulting in behaviors they wouldn't typically engage in.

- **Peer Pressure**: The desire to fit in or be perceived as "experienced" or "adventurous" can sometimes lead individuals to make choices that don't align with their true feelings or comfort levels.

The Societal Impact: STDs, Stigmas, and Societal Perceptions

The repercussions of intimate encounters extend beyond the individuals involved, impacting society at large.

Rise of STDs: A Historical and Contextual Deep Dive

The Ancient Times

STDs are not a new phenomenon. They've existed as long as humans have. Ancient texts, from the Bible to the writings of Hippocrates, contain references that suggest the presence of diseases that could be STDs. Egyptian medical papyri from 1550 B.C. mention symptoms consistent with gonorrhea.

The Renaissance & European Expansion

The most notorious STD, syphilis, made its mark in Europe in the late 15th century. Its rapid spread coincided with the return of French troops from the Italian campaign, leading to it being initially named the "French disease" by Italians, and vice versa. There's still debate among historians whether syphilis was a new import from the Americas or a mutated version of a European bacteria. Regardless, its spread was swift and deadly, with no effective treatment available until the advent of penicillin in the 20th century.

The World Wars Era

During World Wars I and II, the military considered STDs to be a significant threat to troop readiness. Brothels often sprung up around military bases, and the incidence of infections rose dramatically. Military campaigns even aimed to deter soldiers from risky sexual behaviors, equating STDs to enemy sabotage. Post-WWII, with the advent of antibiotics, there was a decline in many STDs, particularly syphilis. However, this relief was temporary.

The Late 20th Century and the HIV/AIDS Epidemic

The latter part of the 20th century witnessed the emergence of HIV/AIDS, which redefined global perceptions of STDs. Originating from Central Africa, HIV/AIDS spread globally, affecting millions. Its severity and the initial lack of any cure or treatment fostered worldwide fear. This led to vast public health campaigns promoting safe sex and increased research into antiviral treatments. Though antiretroviral therapies have since been developed, the disease remains a significant global health concern.

The 21st Century: Rise of Drug-Resistant Strains

While the global health community was focusing on HIV/AIDS, other STDs were quietly evolving. In the last two decades, strains of gonorrhea, chlamydia, and syphilis have emerged that show resistance to standard antibiotic treatments. Casual and unprotected encounters, amplified by the rise of dating apps and changing societal norms, have contributed to increased transmission rates. The rise of these drug-resistant strains poses a significant public health challenge, prompting renewed calls for prevention through education, regular testing, and vaccination where applicable.

Casual and unprotected encounters contribute to the spread of sexually transmitted diseases. With some diseases becoming resistant to treatments, the public health implications are significant.

In understanding the rise and implications of STDs, it's evident that they are intertwined with societal, technological, and medical developments. The challenge ahead lies in balancing the advances that facilitate casual encounters with the knowledge and tools to ensure they're safe.

Stigmas and Shame: A Global Perspective on Intimate Relations

Ancient Civilizations and the Roots of Shame

From the dawn of human civilization, intimate relations, especially outside of sanctioned structures like marriage, often came with societal judgments. In ancient Rome, the Vestal Virgins, priestesses of Vesta, were expected to maintain their chastity for 30 years; failure to do so resulted in being buried alive. Ancient Chinese Confucian teachings emphasized female chastity and fidelity. A woman's worth was often tied to her virtue, which was intrinsically linked to her sexual behavior.

Medieval Europe and Public Shaming

In medieval Europe, chastity belts, designed to prevent sexual intercourse, were reportedly used, although their prevalence might be exaggerated in popular culture. Adulterers, especially women, could be publicly shamed – sometimes by being forced to wear a scarlet letter, as immortalized by Nathaniel Hawthorne's novel. Such practices emphasized the importance of female sexual purity and the societal consequences of its perceived breach.

Colonial and Native Interactions

Colonial powers often imposed their own moral codes upon the nations they colonized, leading to a blending of native customs with imported stigmas. In parts of Africa, India, and other colonized lands, the Victorian values of European powers introduced or reinforced notions of modesty and shame around casual intimate relations.

Asian Societal Norms

In many Asian cultures, premarital or extramarital relations have historically been taboo, with families placing immense importance on virginity before marriage. In some societies, failure to bleed on the wedding night (seen as a sign of virginity) could lead to annulment and public shame. Japan's "love hotels" rose in popularity as a discreet location for couples, reflecting the societal need for privacy and secrecy around intimate relations.

Modern Day and Globalization

The era of globalization and the internet has seen a melding of cultural norms, with Western ideals of freedom and individuality often clashing with traditional values elsewhere. In many Middle Eastern countries, honor and shame are still deeply tied to family reputation, with honor killings tragically persisting. On the other hand, with the spread of Western media and ideals, urban centers in these very regions are experiencing shifts in attitudes towards casual relations, creating generational and urban-rural divides.

Yet, even in progressive societies, remnants of old stigmas linger. Terms like "slut-shaming" have emerged to describe the judgment placed disproportionately on women for their sexual behaviors. The "walk of shame" concept, while humorously portrayed in some media, underscores an enduring double standard: celebration of male conquests versus the shaming of female sexuality.

Even as society progresses, remnants of judgment linger. "The walk of shame" is a term still used, highlighting the judgment placed on individuals, often women, after casual encounters.

Throughout history and across continents, intimate relations outside of societal norms have often been stigmatized. While the specifics vary from one culture to another, the theme of shame, especially directed towards women, is universal. Recognizing this shared history can be the first step towards fostering global empathy and challenging enduring stigmas.

Media portrayal of casual encounters ranges from glorification to demonization. Such mixed messages can create confusion, with individuals feeling pressure to conform to perceived norms while also facing potential judgment.

In a world where intimacy intersects with individual choices, societal norms, and psychological complexities, understanding the multi-faceted aspects of 'the morning after' in the context of sex and relationships is vital. Such understanding paves the way for healthier dialogues, informed choices, and a society that supports rather than judges.

Societal Perceptions and Media Portrayal: An International Tapestry of Judgments and Desires

Ancient Art and Literature

The earliest depictions of intimacy in human culture often had religious or fertility connotations. In ancient Indian art, sensuality was celebrated, as evidenced by the intricate carvings of Khajuraho. Similarly, ancient Greek literature occasionally touched on casual encounters outside of marriage, sometimes with a tone of acceptance, other times with moral undertones.

Renaissance to Victorian Eras

European art from the Renaissance period was filled with sensual depictions, suggesting a more liberal attitude. However, by the Victorian era, Europe's public portrayal of sexuality became more constrained. Despite the apparent conservatism, underground literature and art from this period reveal a society grappling with its desires, reflected in works like the Marquis de Sade's writings.

20th Century Cinema and Music

With the rise of Hollywood in the 20th century, the portrayal of casual encounters in cinema began influencing global perceptions. Initially, strict moral guidelines (like the Hays Code) restricted explicit content. However, the sexual revolution of the 1960s and '70s challenged these norms. Iconic music of the era, from rock 'n' roll to disco, also echoed these liberating sentiments. Yet, movies like "Fatal Attraction" in the 1980s warned of the potential dangers of extramarital affairs, illustrating the conflicted societal views.

Asian Dramas and Films

In regions like South Korea and Japan, television dramas often depict intense romantic relationships, sometimes showing the struggles of individuals against societal expectations. While these dramas might hint at casual relationships, they often emphasize deeper emotional connections, reflecting societal values that prioritize meaningful relationships over fleeting encounters.

Modern Global Media

The proliferation of the internet and streaming platforms has led to a blending of global media norms. Shows like "Sex and the City" from the U.S., which portray casual encounters in a more neutral or even positive light, are available worldwide and influence viewers across different cultures. Conversely, telenovelas from Latin America or Turkish dramas, which might emphasize the sanctity of love and the challenges of betrayal, have found audiences in unexpected places, from Eastern Europe to South Asia.

However, even in the most progressive media depictions, the specter of judgment or consequence for casual relationships frequently appears. Characters often grapple with societal perceptions, reflecting the real-world dichotomy: the natural human desire for connection and exploration against the weight of tradition and judgment.

The dance between media portrayal and societal values is a dynamic one. Media both mirrors and shapes society's attitudes. As international media becomes more accessible, viewers worldwide grapple with the complex tapestry of desires, judgments, and norms. Recognizing the universality of this struggle can help individuals feel less isolated in their experiences and more connected to a shared human journey.

Chapter 5: The Walk of Shame: More Than Just a Metaphor

1. Real-life stories:

a. Maria's Early Morning Escape

Maria, a bright college student from Spain, had always been a bit reserved. When she met Diego at a local festival, they shared an evening filled with laughter, dancing, and mutual attraction. She never expected it to lead to his apartment. But it did. The next morning, she left his place, trying to go unnoticed. The glances she got from passersby, real or imagined, weighed heavily on her. She overheard a whisper, "walk of shame," and felt her face flush. The experience, rather than being a fond memory of a beautiful night, became a source of anxiety for Maria.

b. Samuel's Hasty Exit

In Nigeria, Samuel, a young professional, attended a work event where he connected with a female colleague from another department. One thing led to another, and he found himself at her apartment. The next day, he tried to sneak out, but her neighbors, who recognized him, exchanged knowing glances. At work, hushed conversations and hidden smirks reminded him constantly of that night. The 'walk of shame' wasn't exclusive to women; Samuel felt its weight too.

c. Sameer and Takashi's Night in Tokyo

Sameer, an Indian software engineer, had recently moved to Tokyo for a project. Navigating through the blend of old traditions and futuristic visions of Tokyo, he felt both lost and exhilarated. One evening, after a long day at work, Sameer decided to explore the city's vibrant nightlife in Shinjuku's Ni-chome district, known for its bustling LGBTQ+ scene.

It was in a cozy bar adorned with soft lights and gentle music that Sameer met Takashi, a Japanese graphic designer with a flair for witty conversations. Their connection was palpable: both being from conservative cultures, they discussed the challenges and joys of coming out, the differences in how their respective countries treated LGBTQ+ communities, and their personal journeys of acceptance.

As the night wore on and the drinks kept flowing, the walls Sameer had built around himself started to crumble. Takashi's warm smile and genuine interest made him feel seen in a way he hadn't in a long time. They decided to end the night at Takashi's traditional yet modern Japanese apartment.

Dawn painted Tokyo in soft hues of orange and pink. Sameer, having to leave for an early meeting, quietly gathered his belongings, trying not to wake a peacefully sleeping Takashi. Stepping out into the early morning, he felt a mix of emotions. There was the lingering euphoria from the previous night's connection, the uncertainty of what this meant for their budding relationship, and the slight anxiety of being spotted by neighbors or colleagues.

Walking towards the train station, Sameer couldn't help but feel the weight of the proverbial 'walk of shame' that transcended cultures and genders.

2. The effects on mental health:

The 'walk of shame' has ramifications beyond just an uncomfortable morning. It affects one's self-worth, self-esteem, and mental well-being. For many, it becomes an internal battle between personal choices and societal judgments. Constant worry about the opinions of others can lead to anxiety, stress, and, in severe cases, depressive tendencies. Moreover, it's an internalization of society's views on morality, leading individuals to harshly judge themselves, affecting their confidence and self-image.

3. Reclaiming power: Transforming shame into strength:

Reframing the narrative is essential. Rather than viewing it as a 'walk of shame,' it can be seen as a **walk of experience** or a **walk of choice.** Embracing personal choices and learning from experiences, whether perceived as good or bad, can foster growth. By discussing these experiences openly, without judgment, individuals can help dispel stigmas. When more people start to see it as just another part of the human experience, the weight of the 'walk' lightens. Empowerment comes from embracing one's choices, learning from them, and sharing stories to help others do the same.

Reclaiming Power: Transforming Shame into Strength - Reframing the Narrative Step-by-Step

Step 1: Acknowledgment
Begin by acknowledging the feeling of shame or discomfort.
For example: "I feel ashamed because I believe people are judging me for my choices."

Step 2: Question the Source
Understand where this feeling is coming from.
Ask yourself: "Why do I feel this way? Is it because of my personal beliefs, or is it external pressure from society or peers?"

Step 3: Identify the Positive
Find the positive aspect or learning experience in the situation.
For example: "The connection I had last night was genuine and beautiful. I learned more about myself and what I'm looking for in a relationship."

Step 4: Create a New Story
Transform the narrative from a negative perspective to a positive one.
Instead of: "I shouldn't have stayed over. What will people think?"
Shift to: "I made a choice that felt right to me at the time. What I experienced enriched my understanding of myself and others."

Step 5: Repeat and Affirm
Reinforce this new narrative until it becomes a natural thought process.
Whenever doubt creeps in, remind yourself: "I am in control of my story. I choose to see my experiences as a source of strength, not shame."

Step 6: Share and Connect
Connect with others who might have had similar experiences.
By discussing and sharing, you realize you're not alone. This collective strength can be incredibly empowering.

Step 7: Practice Self-Compassion
Remember to be kind to yourself.

Understanding that everyone makes choices and that they are a part of the human experience helps in extending the same compassion to yourself that you would offer to a friend.

Step 8: Seek External Support
If feelings of shame persist, consider seeking external support.
Professional counseling or support groups can offer tools and perspectives to further help in reframing narratives.

Reframing the narrative is not a one-time action but a continuous process. As with any change in mindset, it takes time, effort, and practice. But with each step, you reclaim a bit more of your power, transforming perceived shame into undeniable strength.

Chapter 6: Abortions: The Ultimate Morning After

1. The Social, Emotional, and Physical Aspects of Abortion:

Abortion is not just a medical procedure but a complex interplay of social, emotional, and physical aspects. Society, fueled by cultural and religious beliefs, often has polarized views on the topic, which can greatly influence a person's experience. The emotional roller coaster accompanying the decision can be compounded by physical aftereffects and potential social stigmatization.

2. Personal stories: The choice, the act, and the aftermath.

a. Aisha and Fatima's Heartrending Choice:

Aisha, a young Muslim woman in a conservative Middle Eastern community, found solace in her childhood friend, Fatima. Their bond deepened over time, evolving into a romantic relationship, which they kept hidden for fear of ostracization. When Aisha discovered she was pregnant after an arranged intimate encounter with a man her parents hoped she'd marry, she was devastated. Fatima, standing firmly by Aisha's side, supported her choice to have an abortion. They traveled to a neighboring country where it was safer for Aisha to undergo the procedure. Their shared ordeal brought them even closer, but they had to navigate their love and the aftermath of the abortion amidst the shadows.

b. Lucia's Decision in Catholic Brazil:

In predominantly Catholic Brazil, Lucia, a single woman in her late twenties, found herself unexpectedly pregnant after a brief relationship. Torn between her religious upbringing and the life she'd planned for herself, Lucia grappled with her decision. Her choice to undergo an abortion was made privately, with only a trusted friend knowing. The emotional aftermath was a journey of reconciling her personal beliefs with her actions.

c. Jay and Priya's Unanticipated Crossroad:

In San Francisco, Jay, a transgender man, and his partner Priya, an Indian immigrant, were thrilled to start a family. However, early medical complications raised concerns about both the baby's and Jay's health.

Facing both medical and social complexities, they made the heart-wrenching decision to terminate the pregnancy. Their journey was one of explaining and justifying their choice in a world that barely understood their love.

3. Navigating the Emotional Landscape Post-abortion:

The days, weeks, and even years post-abortion can be emotionally challenging. Feelings of relief, guilt, sadness, and empowerment can coexist. It's crucial to recognize these emotions without judgment, understanding that each person's experience is unique. Seeking support from professional counselors, understanding friends, or support groups can be instrumental in healing. Importantly, the journey is about finding peace and acceptance, no matter the circumstances surrounding the abortion.

Navigating the Emotional Landscape Post-abortion: A Step-by-Step Guide

Step 1: Recognize and Accept Your Emotions

- **Understanding**: Begin by acknowledging and identifying your emotions without judgment. It's okay to feel a range of emotions from relief to grief, guilt, or even anger.
- **Acceptance**: Give yourself permission to experience these emotions. Understand that they are a natural response to a significant life event.

Step 2: Create a Support System

- **Confide**: Find a trusted friend, family member, or therapist who you can talk to. Sharing your feelings and experiences can provide immense relief.
- **Support Groups**: Consider joining a support group where you can hear and share experiences, providing mutual

understanding and solidarity.

Step 3: Address Cultural and Societal Pressures

- **Information**: Educate yourself about abortion to dispel any myths or misconceptions that your culture might perpetuate.
- **Affirmation**: Remind yourself of your autonomy over your body and decisions. While cultural values are important, your wellbeing is paramount.
- **Distance**: If you feel overwhelmed, consider limiting exposure to judgmental individuals or unsupportive environments temporarily.

Step 4: Self-Care

- **Physical Health**: Ensure you follow post-abortion medical guidance, and schedule regular check-ups.
- **Mental Health**: Engage in activities that help you relax and rejuvenate. This might include reading, meditation, exercise, or pursuing a hobby.
- **Emotional Health**: Journaling can be a powerful tool. Writing down your feelings can offer clarity and serve as an outlet for your emotions.

Step 5: Seek Professional Help if Needed

- **Therapy**: Consider seeing a therapist or counselor who can provide coping strategies tailored to your needs.
- **Helplines**: There are many helplines available where you can talk to someone about your feelings post-abortion, anonymously if preferred.

Step 6: Reflect on Your Values and Beliefs

- **Personal Values**: Take time to reflect on your personal values and beliefs, distinguishing them from those of your culture or society.
- **Evolve**: Understand that beliefs and values can evolve. It's okay to grow and change your views based on your experiences.

Step 7: Rebuild and Look Ahead

- **Plan**: When you're ready, think about your future. This doesn't mean you're forgetting or moving on, but rather integrating the experience into your life story.
- **Empowerment**: Use your experience to empower yourself and possibly others. Sharing your story, when and if you're comfortable, can help destigmatize abortion and offer support to others in similar situations.

Remember, navigating post-abortion emotions amidst cultural and societal pressures can be challenging, but you are not alone. Many resources and communities exist to provide support and understanding. Prioritize your well-being and give yourself the time and space to heal.

Chapter 7: A Universal Perspective

1. 'The Morning After' in Different Cultures: Note: (these perspectives were obtained through personal interviews and are not intended to be a representation or the perception of the entire culture.)

- **Eastern Perspectives**: In traditional Asian cultures, the concept of 'The Morning After' is deeply rooted in values of honor and family prestige. Choices made, especially by women, can significantly impact the family's reputation, leading to a profound sense of guilt or shame.
- **Western Perspectives**: Western societies, particularly in North America and Europe, have been more liberal in their views. The 'Morning After' might be seen more as a personal learning experience rather than a societal issue. However, remnants of conservative views still exist, influencing individual emotions.
- **African & Middle Eastern Perspectives**: In many African and Middle Eastern cultures, the emphasis is on community. Decisions made by an individual can have ripple effects on the broader community's perception, leading to heightened feelings of responsibility and guilt.
- **Latin & South American Perspectives**: With a heavy influence of Catholicism in many of these cultures, moral values play a significant role in how 'The Morning After' is perceived. The intersection of tradition and modernity brings its own set of challenges.

---

2. Historical Perspectives: Choices and Consequences Throughout the Ages:

- **Ancient Civilizations**: From ancient Greece to Egypt, behaviors deemed as immoral were often punished, and the aftermath of such choices held significant societal consequences.

- **Medieval Times**: During this era, societal and religious beliefs were deeply intertwined. Decisions, especially those around relationships, were heavily scrutinized, and the consequences could be severe.

- **Renaissance & Enlightenment**: As societies moved towards reason and individualism, there was a subtle shift. Choices began to be seen in the context of personal freedom, but societal judgment remained.

- **Modern Era**: With the advent of globalization and the spread of information, societal views have rapidly evolved, but the emotional aftermath of certain decisions remains a deeply personal experience.

3. The Role of Society: Judgement, Acceptance, and Change: Why Does Societal Judgment Happen?

Across cultures and ages, society has always played a role in shaping our feelings towards our choices. The fear of judgment can amplify personal guilt or regret.

Societal judgment is an intrinsic aspect of human societies and can be attributed to various factors:

1. Need for Conformity:

At its core, humans are social creatures. From the early days of civilization, adhering to societal norms ensured survival, as individuals who were part of a group were more likely to thrive. This need for conformity has evolved into an innate desire for acceptance within our communities, leading to the establishment of certain 'norms' and 'values'. Those who diverge from these norms might face judgment, as their actions are perceived as threats to societal cohesion.

Life Application: Think of high school cliques or office politics. In such micro-societies, there's often an unspoken code of behavior. Those who act or think differently might face ridicule or exclusion.

2. Fear of the Unknown:

People tend to be wary of what they don't understand. When someone acts in a way that's unfamiliar or against perceived norms, it can lead to discomfort, resulting in judgment as a defense mechanism.

Life Application: Consider cultural misunderstandings. When someone from one cultural background behaves in a way that's unfamiliar to another, it might lead to misjudgments or stereotypes.

3. Power and Control:

Judgment can be a tool for maintaining power dynamics within a society. By creating a rigid framework of what's 'right' and 'wrong', those in power can control and influence the behavior of the masses.

Life Application: Think of historical monarchies or dictatorships where certain behaviors were labeled as treasonous or immoral, not because they were inherently wrong, but because they threatened the power structure.

4. Projection of Personal Insecurities:

Sometimes, individuals judge others as a way to deflect attention from their insecurities. By highlighting someone else's perceived shortcomings, they feel better about their own flaws.

Life Application: Picture a scenario where a person criticizes someone for a mistake at work. Deep down, the critic might be afraid of making a similar mistake and, thus, projects that fear onto someone else.

5. Reinforcement of Identity:

People often identify strongly with their societal groups, be it based on nationality, religion, or any other identifier. Judging those outside of their group can reinforce their identity and create a stronger bond within the group.

Life Application: Sports rivalries are a classic example. Fans might judge or ridicule supporters of rival teams to strengthen their identity and allegiance to their team.

Control and power indeed play significant roles in societal judgment. Those in power often perpetuate judgment to maintain their position and influence over others. By defining and promoting specific norms and values, they can shape the behavior and thinking of the broader society, ensuring that their authority remains unchallenged.

Shifting Towards Acceptance: A Biblical Perspective, World Terms, and Implications

Modern societies are gradually moving towards acceptance and understanding, with many global movements advocating for personal rights and freedoms.

1. Biblical Perspective:

The Bible, across both Old and New Testaments, emphasizes the importance of love, acceptance, and understanding.

- **Golden Rule**: In the Gospel of Matthew 7:12, Jesus states, "So in everything, do to others what you would have them do to you." This foundational teaching encourages acceptance and understanding, implying that we should treat others with the kindness and respect we desire for ourselves.
- **Parable of the Good Samaritan (Luke 10:25-37)**: This story teaches that love and acceptance should extend beyond one's immediate community or cultural group, emphasizing universal love and care.

Life Application: By looking at others through a lens of love, as the Bible encourages, we can create a more accepting and understanding global community, irrespective of cultural or national boundaries.

2. World Terms:

We live in an increasingly globalized world. With the rise of technology, individuals from diverse backgrounds interact more frequently than ever before.

- **Interdependence**: Countries and cultures rely on each other for trade, knowledge exchange, and collaboration on global issues. Acceptance and understanding become crucial for mutual prosperity.
- **Global Issues**: Challenges like climate change, global health crises, and economic disparities require collective efforts. Unity and acceptance are more effective than division and prejudice.

Life Application: Just as teams function better when there's mutual respect and understanding, the global community can address shared challenges more efficiently with a foundation of acceptance.

3. Implications:

- **Enhanced Collaboration**: Shifting towards acceptance can result in better international partnerships. When nations and cultures understand and respect each other, they are more likely to collaborate effectively.
- **Cultural Enrichment**: Acceptance leads to an exchange of ideas and cultures, enriching societies by introducing them to new perspectives, arts, cuisines, and more.

Life Application: Embracing a foreign culture can lead to personal growth. As individuals, when we open ourselves to different ways of thinking, we become more rounded and empathetic.

4. Global Movements Advocating for Personal Rights and Freedoms: Movements like Human Rights Campaigns, Women's Rights Movements, LGBTQ+ rights, and Black Lives Matter, among others, emphasize the importance of acceptance.

- **Biblical Correlation**: Jesus mingled with tax collectors, sinners, and the marginalized, teaching that every individual, irrespective of their status, deserves love and respect.
- **World Implication**: Recognizing individual rights and freedoms means recognizing the inherent worth of every person. Such acceptance not only upholds the dignity of individuals but also fosters a more harmonious society.

Life Application: By supporting global movements that advocate for rights and freedoms, we play our part in creating a world that values every individual, much like the Biblical teachings emphasize the worth of each soul.

In essence, shifting towards acceptance is not just a moral imperative but a practical one. A world founded on acceptance and mutual respect is a world more equipped to face its challenges, celebrate its diversity, and ensure a brighter future for all its inhabitants.

The Continuous Evolution: Cultivating a World Beyond Social Norms

Understanding the Current Landscape:

Before we delve into creating a revolution, it's essential to grasp the current societal framework. Over time, societies have transitioned from rigid norms and hierarchies to more fluid structures. With globalization and the internet, there's been an increased exposure to diverse ideas, cultures, and lifestyles. This constant evolution lays the groundwork for a generation that can further diminish, or even eliminate, stringent social norms.

Step-by-Step Guide to Cultivating the Call:

1. Educate Early and Broadly:

Action: Integrate global history, cultures, and current affairs into school curriculums.

Result: A well-informed younger generation that understands and respects global diversities.

2. Promote Cross-Cultural Exchanges:

Action: Encourage student exchange programs, international internships, and global collaborative projects.

Result: Direct exposure to different societies can challenge and reshape pre-existing notions, fostering mutual respect.

3. Advocate for Media Responsibility:

Action: Engage media houses to represent diverse characters, cultures, and stories accurately.

Result: Positive and diverse representation can help normalize various lifestyles, reducing stereotypes.

4. Establish Safe Spaces:

Action: Create environments where people can openly discuss their experiences, fears, and aspirations without judgment.

Result: Enhances empathy, understanding, and solidarity among individuals from different walks of life.

5. Leverage Technology:

Action: Utilize virtual reality, AI, and online platforms to simulate experiences and challenges faced by different individuals.

Result: By walking a mile in someone's virtual shoes, individuals can develop a more profound empathy and understanding.

6. Encourage Personal Reflection:

Action: Advocate for mindfulness practices, journaling, and self-awareness exercises.

Result: When individuals reflect on their biases and beliefs, they're more likely to question and change them.

7. Collaborate on Global Initiatives:

Action: Support global movements advocating for personal rights, freedoms, and inclusivity.

Result: A unified global stand can effectively challenge and change deep-rooted societal norms.

8. Celebrate Differences:

Action: Organize cultural festivals, parades, and global food days.

Result: Celebrating diverse cultures in a positive light can challenge pre-existing prejudices.

9. Support Mental Health:

Action: Make mental health resources easily accessible and normalize seeking help.

Result: By addressing personal traumas and insecurities, individuals can be more open to understanding and accepting others.

10. Foster Continuous Learning:

Action: Promote lifelong learning through workshops, seminars, and online courses on diverse topics.

Result: As individuals continue to learn and grow, they can adapt to evolving societal structures and promote acceptance.

As societies grow and evolve, so do their norms and values. With increased global interactions, there's hope for a more understanding and supportive world where individuals can navigate their 'Morning After' with resilience and empathy.

By following this roadmap, societies can usher in a new era, where individuals are not bound by conventional norms but are free to define their path. The continuous evolution will be characterized by empathy, understanding, and acceptance, providing everyone the freedom to navigate their 'Morning After' with grace and resilience.

Chapter 8: Transformation & Healing

1. Recognizing the Need for Change:

Biblical Perspective:

The story of Saul's conversion to Paul in the New Testament is an iconic example of recognizing the need for change. Saul, once a persecutor of Christians, has a life-altering encounter on the road to Damascus. This experience highlights the potential for radical transformation when one is confronted with their actions.

World View & Story:

Anna, a young woman from Sweden, recognized the toxic patterns in her life after a series of unfortunate events, much like Saul's enlightenment. Her life was characterized by substance abuse and negligence towards her family. However, a near-death experience made her confront her choices, realizing she needed a significant change.

2. The Power of Self-forgiveness:

Biblical Perspective:

In the parable of the prodigal son (Luke 15:11-32), a wayward son squanders his inheritance but decides to return home, expecting scorn. Instead, he's received with unconditional love and forgiveness by his father. The story underscores the importance of self-forgiveness before seeking forgiveness from others.

World View & Story:

Carlos, hailing from Mexico, battled with guilt from past mistakes, feeling he could never rectify them. Drawing inspiration from the prodigal son, he embarked on a journey of self-forgiveness, understanding that true healing begins from within.

3. Rehabilitation and Support Systems:

Biblical Perspective:

The healing of the paralyzed man in Mark 2:1-12 is a testament to the power of community. Friends of the paralyzed man lower him through a roof to be healed by Jesus. This story signifies that sometimes, healing requires support from those around us.

World View & Story:

Nina, a Filipino woman, found herself lost in a cycle of bad relationships and low self-worth. It was her close-knit group of friends who, seeing her struggle, connected her with therapy and support groups. Like the paralyzed man, it was her community that paved the way to her healing.

4. Empowerment: Turning Regret into Lessons and Growth:

Biblical Perspective:

Peter's denial of Jesus during his trials is a tale of regret turned into empowerment. Though Peter denied Jesus thrice, he later became a foundational figure in the early church. His story teaches that past mistakes don't define us; it's how we grow from them.

World View & Story:

Ade, from Nigeria, had always regretted not pursuing higher education and felt stuck in a dead-end job. Reminded of Peter's growth from regret, he decided to turn his life around. At 40, Ade returned to school, proving that it's never too late to transform regrets into stepping stones for growth.

Through these biblical perspectives and worldly views, it becomes evident that transformation and healing are attainable. By recognizing the need for change, embracing self-forgiveness, relying on supportive communities, and leveraging regrets as lessons, individuals can redefine their 'Morning After' into a promising dawn of new beginnings.

Chapter 9: Strategies for Avoiding 'The Morning After'

Step by Step in Building Self-Awareness:
Building self-awareness is a crucial step towards personal growth and understanding. Here is a step-by-step guide to help you cultivate self-awareness:

Step 1: Self-Reflection

- Dedicate quiet time each day to reflect on your thoughts, emotions, and behaviors.
- Ask yourself questions like, "Why did I react that way?" or "What triggered that emotion?"
- Keep a journal to jot down your thoughts and feelings, which can provide insights into patterns over time.

Step 2: Seek Feedback

- Talk to trusted friends, family, or colleagues and ask them for honest feedback about your behaviors and patterns.
- Be open to criticism, recognizing that it can be a tool for growth.

Step 3: Practice Mindfulness and Meditation

- Engage in practices that help you stay present and focused on the current moment.
- Mindfulness helps in recognizing and accepting feelings, thoughts, and sensations in the present moment.

Step 4: Set Clear Boundaries

- Understand what you can tolerate and accept, both mentally and emotionally.
- By setting boundaries, you become more aware of when they are crossed, which can lead to greater self-understanding.

Step 5: Understand Your Core Values

- Identify what is truly important to you, what values drive your actions and decisions.
- Aligning your actions with your values can lead to a more coherent sense of self.

Step 6: Take Personality Tests

- Tools like the Myers-Briggs Type Indicator or the Enneagram can provide insights into your personality type and how you relate to the world.

Step 7: Stay Curious

- Constantly ask yourself questions. Challenge your beliefs and assumptions.
- The more you question, the more you'll uncover about yourself.

Step 8: Seek Professional Guidance

- Consider seeing a therapist or counselor who can provide expert tools and strategies to help in building self-awareness.

Step 9: Accept Yourself

- Understand that everyone has strengths and weaknesses. Embrace them.
- Accepting yourself, warts and all, is a key component of self-awareness.

Step 10: Set Goals and Monitor Progress

- Once you understand more about yourself, set personal goals.
- Regularly check in on your progress. Celebrate your achievements and learn from your setbacks.

Building self-awareness is an ongoing journey. As you grow and change, it's essential to continually revisit and adjust your understanding of yourself. Celebrate the small wins along the way and be patient with yourself. With dedication and persistence, the path to self-awareness will lead to a more fulfilled and balanced life.

Now read this as your inner self:

"I... I often feel like I'm looking at myself from the outside, unable to understand why I do certain things, why I hurt so much... But I've come to realize... sniffs ...that true healing begins with knowing oneself. Building self-awareness isn't just about confronting the demons of the past, but it's about accepting them. It's like standing in front of a mirror, even if the reflection shows scars and imperfections. Every tear I shed, every painful memory I revisit, it's a step closer to understanding the 'why' behind my actions. It's my first step towards change... towards healing."

2. Step by Step Healthy Coping Mechanisms:

Healthy coping mechanisms are essential for managing stress, trauma, or other emotional challenges. Developing these skills can significantly enhance one's mental and emotional well-being. Here's a step-by-step guide to identifying and cultivating healthy coping strategies:

Step 1: Self-assessment

- Begin by reflecting on your current coping mechanisms. Are they constructive or destructive?
- Recognize patterns or triggers that lead you to rely on unhealthy coping strategies, such as substance abuse, overeating, or avoidance.

Step 2: Research

- Educate yourself about various healthy coping techniques. There are countless resources, both online and offline, that discuss the topic.

Step 3: Explore Different Techniques

- Try out various methods to determine which resonates most with you. Here are some to consider:
    - Deep breathing exercises.
    - Physical activity (e.g., walking, yoga, dancing).
    - Meditation or mindfulness practices.
    - Journaling or expressive writing.
    - Engaging in hobbies or activities you love.

Step 4: Seek Professional Help

- Consider consulting a therapist or counselor. They can offer guidance tailored to your specific challenges and needs.

Step 5: Build a Support System

- Surround yourself with supportive friends or family who understand and respect your journey toward cultivating healthier coping mechanisms.
- Consider joining a support group, where you can learn from others' experiences.

Step 6: Limit Exposure to Triggers

- If certain environments or situations exacerbate your stress or negative emotions, minimize your exposure to them, if possible.

Step 7: Set Boundaries

- Learn to say "no" when necessary. It's okay to prioritize your mental and emotional well-being.

Step 8: Practice Regularly

- Like any skill, the more you practice your coping strategies, the more effective they will become. Make them a routine part of your life.

Step 9: Educate Others

- As you learn more about healthy coping mechanisms, share your knowledge with friends or loved ones who might also benefit.

Step 10: Review and Adjust

- Periodically assess how well your coping techniques are working. Be open to adjusting or trying new strategies as needed.

Identifying Healthy Coping Mechanisms:

1. **Positive Impact**: A healthy coping mechanism should make you feel better, not worse. It should bring relief without causing harm in the long run.
2. **Consistent Results**: Over time, using the coping strategy should lead to consistently positive outcomes, such as reduced stress or better emotional management.
3. **No Harm to Self or Others**: The strategy should not harm you physically, mentally, or emotionally, nor should it harm those around you.
4. **Feels Right**: Trust your intuition. If a coping mechanism feels

forced or unnatural, it might not be the best fit for you.

5. **Endorsement by Professionals**: Therapists, counselors, or other mental health professionals can validate if a coping strategy is beneficial.

Remember, everyone is unique, so what works for one person might not work for another. It's essential to find what suits you best and integrate it into your daily life. As you cultivate and refine your coping mechanisms, you'll be better equipped to handle life's challenges in a healthy and resilient manner.

Now read this as your inner self:

As tears stream down, "For the longest time, every hurt, every pain... I tried to numb it. And God knows, I've tried everything – distractions, substances, running away. But they were just... temporary fixes. They didn't help. They just masked the pain, waiting to resurface. So I've been learning, bit by bit, to find healthier ways to cope. Ways that heal instead of harm. Whether it's talking to someone, writing, or simply breathing in and out on a rough day... I'm learning to face my pain head-on. And every time I choose these healthier paths, I feel a little stronger. It's a slow journey, but one I'm committed to making."*

Step by Step Making Informed Choices: Balancing Emotion with Logic:

Understanding how to make informed decisions by balancing emotion with logic is crucial for leading a fulfilling life. While emotion provides the color and texture of our experiences, logic ensures that we make choices in our best interests.

Step 1: Acknowledge Your Emotions

- Recognize the emotions you are feeling without judgment.
- Understand that emotions are natural and provide valuable information about how you relate to situations.

Step 2: Reflect on the Source

- Ask yourself why you're feeling a particular way. Is it an experience influencing your current emotions, or is it directly related to the situation at hand?

Step 3: Delay Decision Making (if possible)

- If you're in an emotionally charged state, consider delaying your decision until you've had a chance to calm down and evaluate the situation logically.

Step 4: Seek Outside Perspectives

- Sometimes, discussing your situation with a trusted friend, family member, or mentor can provide new insights. They might see things from a logical viewpoint that you haven't considered.

Step 5: List Pros and Cons

- Write down the potential benefits and drawbacks of your decision. This simple exercise can help clarify the situation and balance emotional reactions with logical considerations.

Step 6: Visualize Outcomes

- Consider the best-case, worst-case, and most likely scenarios of your decision. How do you feel about each outcome?

Step 7: Trust Your Gut, but Verify

- Intuition is essential but ensure that it's aligned with logic. Validate your gut feelings with evidence and reason.

Step 8: Make the Decision

- Once you've weighed both the emotional and logical aspects, make your choice confidently.

Step 9: Reflect and Adjust

- After some time has passed, review your decision. Did it have the desired outcome? Use this as a learning experience for future choices.

Balancing Emotion and Logic Across Cultures

Every culture has its unique set of values, norms, and traditions, which can influence how emotions and logic are perceived and balanced:

1. **Collectivist Cultures**: These cultures often prioritize the group over the individual. Emotional decisions might consider the feelings and needs of the family or community, while logic might involve how decisions impact group harmony.

2. **Individualistic Cultures**: Here, the focus is more on individual rights and personal freedom. Logic often aligns with personal benefit, while emotions are more centered on individual feelings and experiences.

3. **High Context Cultures**: In cultures like Japan or many Arab nations, non-verbal cues and implied context hold significant meaning. Balancing emotion and logic may involve reading between the lines and understanding unspoken sentiments.

4. **Low Context Cultures**: Cultures like the U.S. or Germany often prioritize explicit communication. Logic may manifest in clear arguments and evidence, while emotions might be expressed openly.

5. **Spiritual and Religious Influences**: In many cultures, spiritual or religious beliefs play a crucial role in decision-making. Emotion might be intertwined with spiritual feelings, while logic could be aligned with religious teachings or scriptures.

Mitigating the influence of deeply ingrained spiritual or religious beliefs on one's decision-making is a sensitive topic. The goal is not to diminish or undermine these beliefs but to allow an individual the freedom to make choices that are best for them, even if they diverge from cultural or religious norms. Here's a guide to encourage personal autonomy while respecting spiritual and religious beliefs:

1. Educate and Empower

- **Self-awareness**: Begin by encouraging individuals to develop self-awareness. They should understand the basis of their beliefs, distinguishing between personal convictions and teachings they've been conditioned to accept without question.
- **Access to diverse perspectives**: Expose individuals to a wide range of beliefs and philosophies. Reading, traveling, or attending lectures can broaden horizons and inspire critical thinking.

2. Encourage Dialogue

- **Open discussions**: Create safe spaces for individuals to discuss their feelings, beliefs, and doubts without fear of judgment. Open dialogue can be therapeutic and can provide clarity.
- **Professional counseling**: For those who feel profoundly conflicted, speaking with a therapist, especially one familiar with spiritual or religious counseling, can be beneficial.

3. Cultivate Personal Values

- **Value assessment**: Encourage individuals to identify and list their personal values. While spiritual and religious beliefs will play a role, other experiences and knowledge can shape these values.
- **Decision-making exercises**: Encourage role-playing or hypothetical scenarios to practice decision-making that aligns with personal values.

4. Promote Balance

- **Mindfulness and meditation**: Techniques like mindfulness meditation can help individuals connect with their inner feelings and thoughts, allowing for a clearer understanding of their personal beliefs versus external influences.

- **Analytical tools**: Teach logical tools and strategies to analyze decisions critically. This can include pros-and-cons lists, risk assessments, or even simple discussions that weigh emotions against logic.

5. Respect and Reassurance

- **Validate feelings**: Regardless of one's choice, it's essential to validate their feelings and ensure they know they're understood and respected.
- **Community support**: Connect individuals with supportive communities or groups, especially if they feel isolated from their previous spiritual or religious group due to their choices.

Empowering individuals to make autonomous decisions while navigating the influence of spiritual and religious beliefs is a journey. With the right support, tools, and understanding, one can find a balance that respects tradition and personal autonomy.

To successfully balance emotion with logic across cultures, one should be culturally sensitive, open-minded, and willing to adapt. Understanding the cultural nuances related to decision-making can lead to more informed and harmonious choices in diverse settings.

Now read this as your inner self:

"You know, it's so hard... voice breaks ...especially when emotions run high. I've often found myself swept away by them, leading me to make impulsive decisions. Decisions I later regret. But I've begun to see the power of pause. Taking that deep breath, allowing myself to feel but also... to think. Balancing my emotions with logic. It's not about negating what I feel but understanding the why and considering the consequences. I still stumble, and sometimes the weight of emotions pulls me down, but every day I strive, with every tear I shed, to make informed choices... choices that are right for my well-being."

Hearing the pain, the growth, and the hope in these heartfelt confessions, it's evident that the journey of healing and transformation is deeply personal and filled with valleys and peaks. But with every step, every tear, there's progress and the promise of a better tomorrow.

Chapter 10: Conclusion

Empathy, Understanding, and Collective Growth: A Step-by-Step Guide

1. Self-reflection: Begin Within

- **Personal Journaling**: Daily writing can help articulate feelings, concerns, and hopes. Over time, this builds awareness about one's biases and judgments.
- **Mindfulness Meditation**: Take moments to sit quietly and reflect on your feelings, thoughts, and responses to various situations. This helps in grounding oneself and understanding one's reactions better.

Life Application: Before reacting to a situation, pause and introspect. Why do you feel this way? Is it based on past experiences or judgments? Practicing this regularly can lead to more empathetic responses.

2. Active Listening: Hear and Understand

- **Avoid Interruptions**: When someone is speaking, ensure you're genuinely listening without formulating your response in your mind.
- **Reflect**: After listening, paraphrase what you heard to confirm understanding.

Life Application: In daily conversations, especially during disagreements, practice active listening. This not only reduces misunderstandings but also strengthens relationships.

3. Educate Yourself: Broaden Horizons

- **Diverse Reading**: Read books, articles, or journals from cultures or perspectives different from your own.
- **Engage in Cultural Events**: Attend events or gatherings which expose you to diverse worldviews.

Life Application: Once a month, try to engage with content or an event that's outside of your cultural comfort zone.

4. Foster Community Growth: Collective Enlightenment

- **Community Discussions**: Organize or attend group discussions on sensitive or relevant topics. This can help in understanding varied perspectives.
- **Promote Inclusive Activities**: Organize events that bring diverse groups together.

Life Application: Collaborate with local community centers to host monthly 'cultural exchange' events.

5. Empower Others: Pay it Forward

- **Share Your Journey**: Talk about your experiences and the benefits of being more empathetic and understanding.
- **Mentorship**: Guide others on this path. Mentor someone seeking to grow in empathy.

Life Application: Volunteer in mentorship programs or start one if it doesn't exist.

Conclusion: The Transformative Power of Reflection

Taking time to reflect on one's actions, beliefs, and biases is transformative. It's through reflection that growth happens. As individuals cultivate empathy and understanding, societies at large will begin to shift. This collective growth moves the world towards a more harmonious future.

Embracing empathy and understanding doesn't just benefit the individual; it enriches society. When one person transforms, it creates ripples, inspiring others to grow and change. The path to a more empathetic world begins with reflection, active efforts, and the belief that change is possible.

Chapter 11: Appendices

Resources for Help and Support

Hotlines: A list of 24/7 hotlines catering to various needs, including mental health, addiction, and emotional support, specific to different countries.

Therapeutic Centers: Information on therapy and counseling centers, which offer sliding scale fees based on financial need.

Online Platforms: Websites and apps that provide guided meditations, emotional support, forums for sharing stories, and other tools for emotional and mental well-being.

Community Groups: Local support groups focusing on specific issues like addiction, trauma, or personal growth. Attendees can share experiences and coping strategies in a safe environment.

Further Readings:

"The Art of Empathy" **by Karla McLaren**: An exploration of the emotional intelligence of empathy and its role in understanding and connecting with others.

"The Road Less Traveled" **by M. Scott Peck**: A classic work on understanding the nature of love, life, and spiritual growth.

"Sapiens: A Brief History of Humankind" **by Yuval Noah Harari**: Offers a sweeping narrative of human history, shedding light on societal norms and values across different cultures and eras.

"The Gifts of Imperfection" **by Brené Brown**: A guide to embracing vulnerability and worthiness, delving into the power of love, belonging, and being enough.

Author Insights

The journey in writing this book has been transformative. I've been a silent observer of numerous 'Morning After' moments, both in my own life and in the lives of those around me. It's through these observations that I've come to realize the profound impact of societal norms and judgments on individual choices and emotions.

*From the diverse stories of the individuals mentioned **(but names changed for confidentiality)** to the emotional challenges faced by so many, the process has been both enlightening and humbling. Every chapter reinforced the fact that while experiences may differ, the undercurrent of emotions, challenges, and the human need for acceptance and understanding remain universal.*

One of the most profound experiences was engaging with various cultures and understanding the role of societal norms, spirituality, and religious beliefs in shaping decisions and inducing feelings of shame or regret. It's been an incredible journey of understanding human nature in all its complexity. To anyone reading, I hope you find solace in knowing you're not alone. Your 'Morning After' might be unique, but the emotions, challenges, and growth potentials are shared by many. I hope this work serves as a guide to understanding, acceptance, and, most importantly, self-love.

Did you love *The Morning After*? Then you should read *The Harvest is Ripe, but the Laborers are Few": A Biblical Perspective on Calling the Called*[1] by Minister Jeremy B. Sims!

[2]

In the vast tapestry of the Bible, the theme of God's call to individuals and the metaphor of the harvest stand out with profound significance. From the Old Testament prophets to Jesus' parables, the call to harvest souls for God's kingdom remains urgent and compelling. This exploration delves deep into the biblical foundations of calling, examining the journeys of figures like Moses, Esther, and Paul. We witness their struggles, obedience, and the fruits of heeding the call. Moreover, we're challenged to reflect upon our own roles in the spiritual harvest. How do we discern God's voice amidst life's clamor? How can communities of faith support each other in this divine mission? And, in

---

1. https://books2read.com/u/mgR6PR

2. https://books2read.com/u/mgR6PR

a world brimming with distractions, how do we remain faithful laborers in God's vineyard? By understanding the past, we gain insights and tools for today's harvest, realizing that our roles in this eternal mission are both a privilege and a responsibility.

Also by Jeremy B. Sims

Awakened Wellness: Are YOU Spiritually Motivated Yet?
Stop Blaming the Adversary: It's You!
From Milk to Meat: The Journey of Spiritual Maturity
The Morning After